ULTIMATE MANGA
HOW TO DRAW
FANTASY MANGA

Marc Powell and David Neal

PowerKiDS press™

New York

WITH THANKS TO ODA, STEVE, AILIN, AND PAT

Published in 2016 by **The Rosen Publishing Group**
29 East 21st Street, New York, NY 10010

Text by Jack Hawkins
Edited by Jack Hawkins
Designed by Dynamo Ltd and Emma Randall
Cover design by Notion Design
Illustrations by Marc Powell and David Neal

Cataloging-in-Publication Data
Powell, Marc.
How to draw fantasy manga / by Marc Powell and David Neal.
p. cm. — (Ultimate manga)
Includes index.
ISBN 978-1-4994-1142-3 (pbk.)
ISBN 978-1-4994-1152-2 (6 pack)
ISBN 978-1-4994-1176-8 (library binding)
1. Comic books, strips, etc. — Japan — Technique — Juvenile literature.
2. Drawing — Technique — Juvenile literature. 3. Fantasy in art — Juvenile literature.
I. Title.
NC1764.5.J3 P694 2016
741.5'1—d23

Manufactured in the United States of America
CPSIA Compliance Information: Batch WS15PK: For Further Information
contact Rosen Publishing, New York, New York at 1-800-237-9932

CONTENTS

HOW TO USE THIS BOOK

The drawings in this book have been built up in seven stages. Each stage uses lines of a different color so you can see the new layer clearly. Of course, you don't have to use different colors in your work. Use a pencil for the first four stages so you can get your drawing right before moving on to the inking and coloring stages.

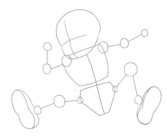

Stage 1: Green lines
This is the basic stick figure of your character.

Stage 2: Red lines
The next step is to flesh out the simple stick figure.

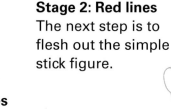

Stage 3: Blue lines
Then finish the basic shape and add in extra details.

Stage 4: Black lines
Add in clothes and any accessories.

Stage 5: Inks
The inking stage will give you a final line drawing.

Stage 6: Colors
"Flat" coloring uses lighter shades to set the base colors of your character.

Stage 7: Shading
Add shadows for light sources, and use darker colors to add depth to your character.

BASIC TOOLS

You don't need lots of complicated, expensive tools for your manga images – many of them are available from a good stationery shop. The others can be found in any art supplies store, or online.

PENCILS

These are probably the most important tool for any artist. It's important to find a type of pencil you are comfortable with, since you will be spending a lot of time using it.

Graphite

You will be accustomed to using graphite pencils – they are the familiar wood-encased "lead" pencils. They are available in a variety of densities from the softest, 9B, right up to the hardest, 9H. Hard pencils last longer and are less likely to smudge on the paper. Most artists use an HB (#2) pencil, which falls in the middle of the density scale.

Mechanical pencils

Also known as propelling pencils, these contain a length of lead that can be replaced. The leads are available in the same densities as graphite pencils. The great advantage of mechanical pencils over graphite is that you never have to sharpen them – you simply extend more lead as it wears down.

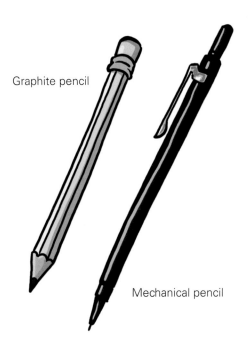

Graphite pencil

Mechanical pencil

Marker

Ballpoint pen

INKING PENS

After you have penciled your piece of artwork, you will need to ink the line to give a sharp, solid image.

Ballpoint pens

Standard ballpoint pens are ideal for lining your piece. However, their quality varies, as does their delivery of ink. A single good-quality ballpoint pen is better than a collection of cheap ones.

Marker pens

Standard marker pens of varying thicknesses are ideal for coloring and shading your artworks. They provide a steady, consistent supply of ink, and can be used to build layers of color by re-inking the same area. They are the tools most frequently used for manga coloring.

POWERFUL WIZARD

Japanese folktales are full of wizards with magical powers. They gain their abilities from their mystical martial arts skills or pacts with spirits. This character could pass for a friendly old man, but cross him and his wizardry will be unleashed!

STEP 1
Draw a basic stick figure with his arms raised from the elbow and his right foot resting on a rock. We are looking up at him, so his eyeline is higher than normal.

STEP 2
Use cylinder shapes to give form to your character's arms and legs. Draw the lines to mark the sides of his neck and sketch in the basic shapes of his hands. His left hand is in the foreground, so it is larger than the right.

STEP 3
Add your character's basic anatomical details and facial features. Draw his hands with the palms facing forwards. Add some detail to the rock beneath his foot.

STEP 4
Give your character a large mustache and complete his facial features, adding shading under his chin. Draw his clothing and shoes.

STEP 5

Use your lining pen to go over the lines that will
be visible in the finished drawing and erase any
pencil lines. Add details to the wizard's clothes
and shading to his face, neck, and arms.

ARTIST'S TIP

Remember that you can make
final adjustments to the body,
clothes and accessories at
your final pencil stage. The
construction steps are guides
to help you reach this stage.

STEP 6
Add the base colors. The use of muted tones helps to make his bright red sash stand out.

STEP 7
Use color to add more shading to your image and draw the yellow electrical flashes between the wizard's hands.

UNDERWORLD MONSTER

No fantasy story would be complete without a supernatural being to cause trouble for the heroes. Our monster is powerful and frightening, so how will your heroes react? A single monster would be bad enough, but now imagine a whole pack . . . .

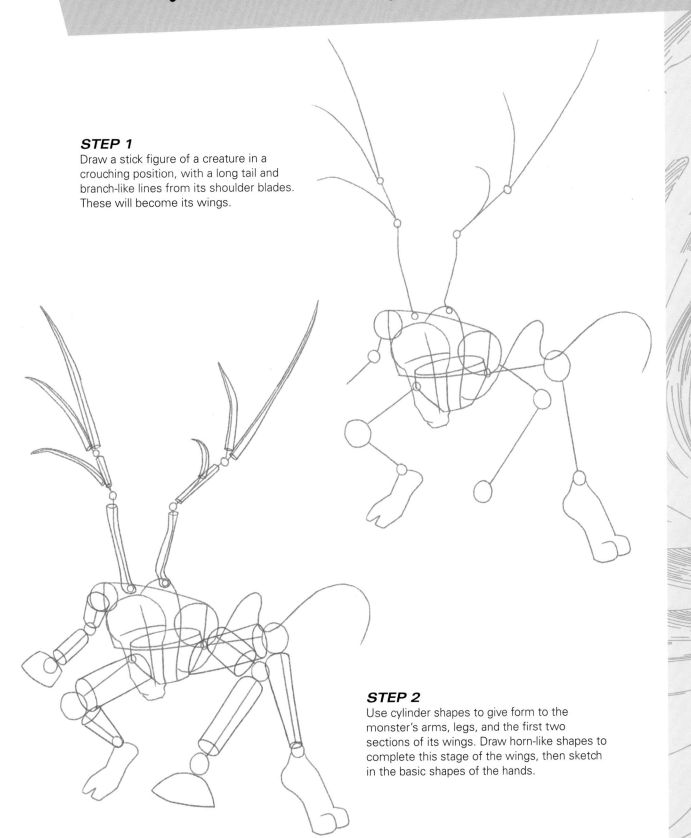

STEP 1
Draw a stick figure of a creature in a crouching position, with a long tail and branch-like lines from its shoulder blades. These will become its wings.

STEP 2
Use cylinder shapes to give form to the monster's arms, legs, and the first two sections of its wings. Draw horn-like shapes to complete this stage of the wings, then sketch in the basic shapes of the hands.

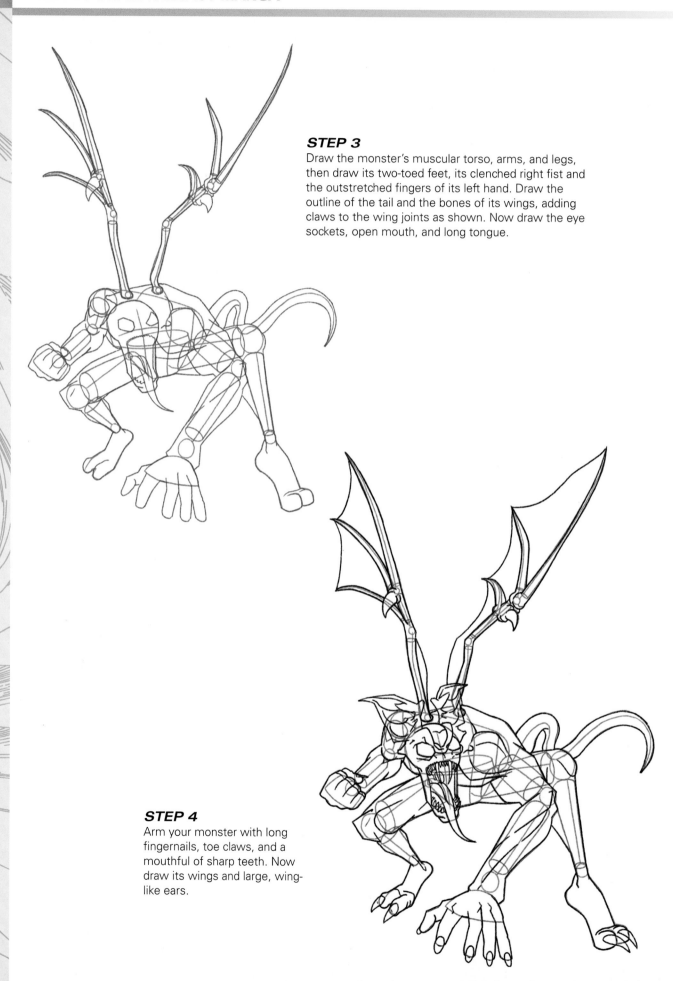

STEP 3
Draw the monster's muscular torso, arms, and legs, then draw its two-toed feet, its clenched right fist and the outstretched fingers of its left hand. Draw the outline of the tail and the bones of its wings, adding claws to the wing joints as shown. Now draw the eye sockets, open mouth, and long tongue.

STEP 4
Arm your monster with long fingernails, toe claws, and a mouthful of sharp teeth. Now draw its wings and large, wing-like ears.

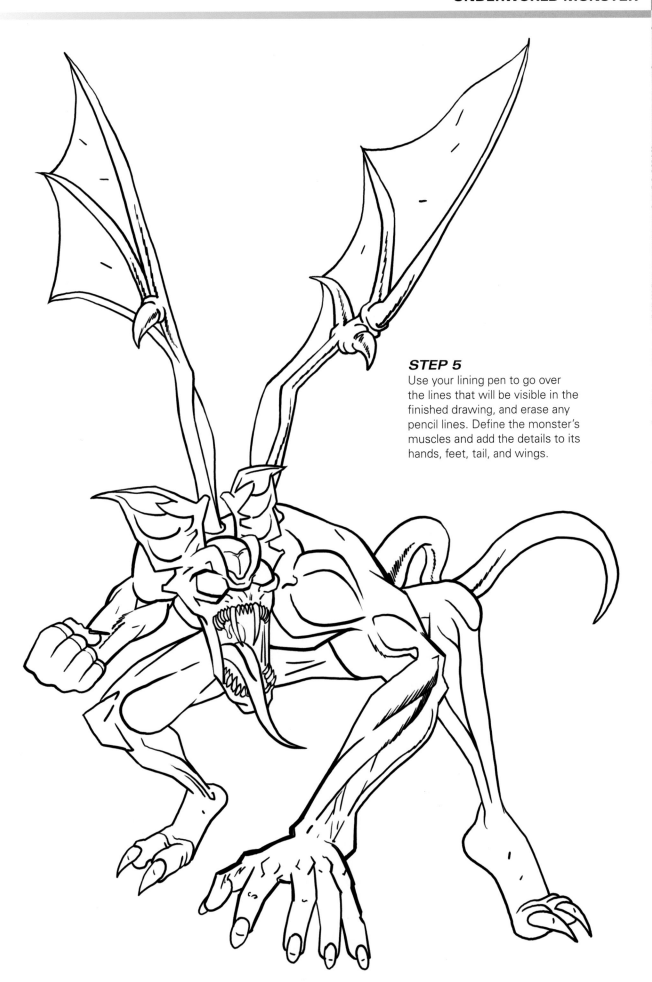

STEP 5
Use your lining pen to go over the lines that will be visible in the finished drawing, and erase any pencil lines. Define the monster's muscles and add the details to its hands, feet, tail, and wings.

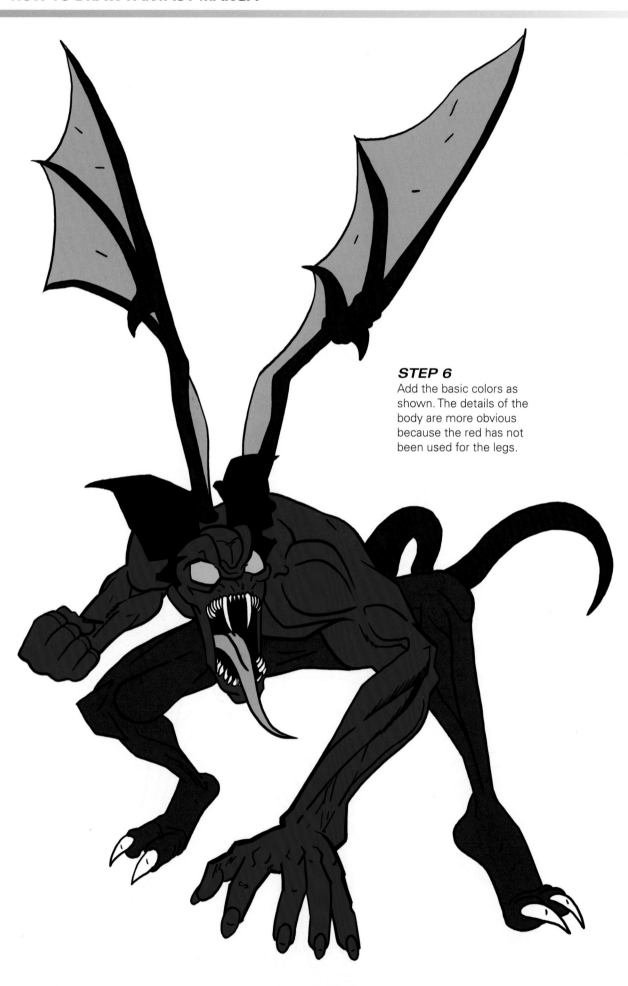

STEP 6

Add the basic colors as shown. The details of the body are more obvious because the red has not been used for the legs.

STEP 7
Darker shades of the base red have been used to add shadows. These add definition to the drawing and give a menacing character even more bite.

SPECIAL EFFECTS

There's no limit to what you can allow your characters to do in a fantasy world. Giving your creations some special powers is a great way to set them apart from the ordinary characters in your story. Think about how you will show these powers in your drawings.

Now you see me . . .

Let's take a look at giving your characters some invisibility skills. Starting with the basic head shape, plot out the shape of the disappearing body by using a line like this.

Draw in the head and shoulders and then thicken the squiggle line to help make the crackle effect of the magic.

Complete the detail of the head and add shading to the squiggle. Electrical bolt effects can be created by extending the line in places.

Finish the shading on the head and shoulders. Add small patches of shading for extra crackle effects. Particles of debris help complete the impression of chaos.

Putting in focus lines and sound effects will add further drama.

Unleash nature

You will probably want to give a character one of the more impressive elemental powers. Let's look at some options.

Fire

Plan the shape and trajectory of your fireball with a basic sketch. The darker inner section will eventually represent the burning core.

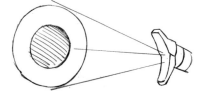

Using your basic sketch, round off the front of the fireball. Show small flames flowing down the edges of the fireball away from the direction of travel.

Strengthen the outer line and add dark shaded patches to represent burning bits and charred embers within the central core. Emphasize the drama by adding extreme shadows to the fireball's point of origin . . . in this case, the dragon's head!

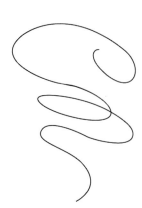

Water

Water is a flowing element, so a curling line is an excellent place to start when creating your water blast. Keep it fluid and avoid any sharp angles in your curves.

Duplicate your original line to create the rest of the water blast. Think of the water as a piece of elastic that can twist and bend upon itself, but which will not break.

Use shading to give texture to your water. Add drops of flying water and small splashes wherever the water changes direction.

DRAGON

No other fantasy creature is quite as impressive as a dragon. The look of your dragon will determine the impression it makes, so think carefully about its size and shape. We have given this dragon an upright posture and wolf-like features.

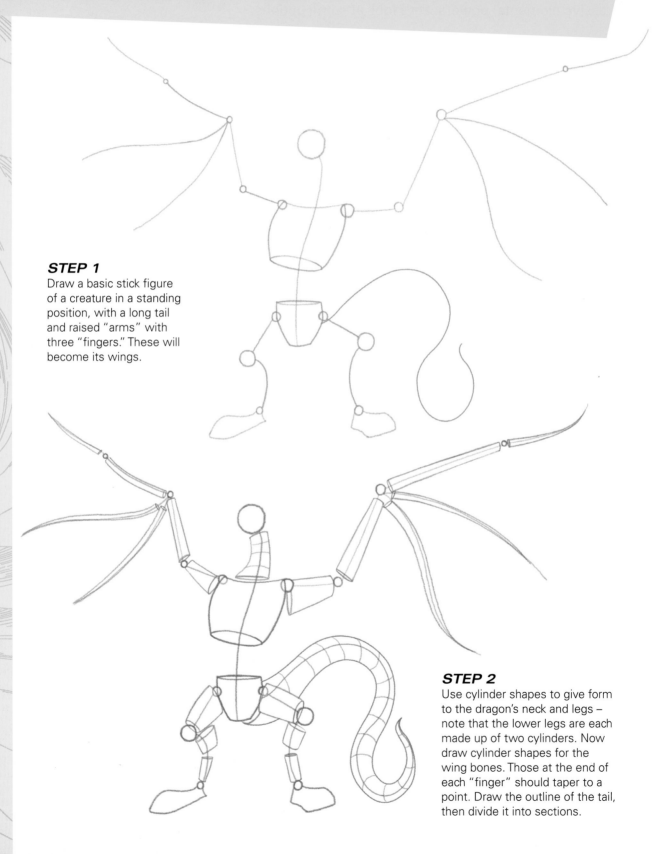

STEP 1
Draw a basic stick figure of a creature in a standing position, with a long tail and raised "arms" with three "fingers." These will become its wings.

STEP 2
Use cylinder shapes to give form to the dragon's neck and legs – note that the lower legs are each made up of two cylinders. Now draw cylinder shapes for the wing bones. Those at the end of each "finger" should taper to a point. Draw the outline of the tail, then divide it into sections.

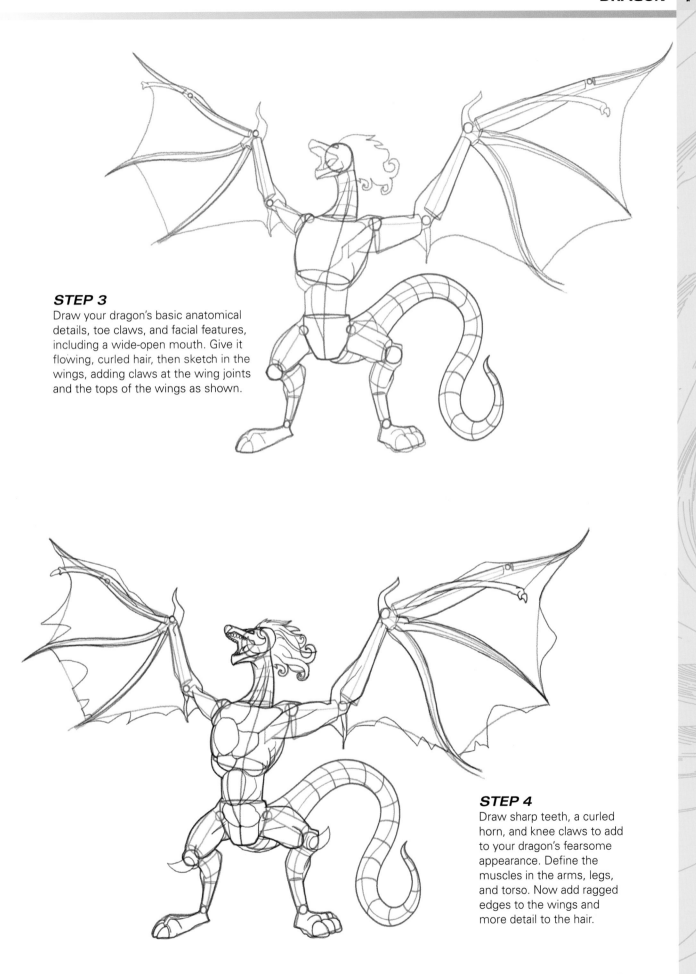

STEP 3

Draw your dragon's basic anatomical details, toe claws, and facial features, including a wide-open mouth. Give it flowing, curled hair, then sketch in the wings, adding claws at the wing joints and the tops of the wings as shown.

STEP 4

Draw sharp teeth, a curled horn, and knee claws to add to your dragon's fearsome appearance. Define the muscles in the arms, legs, and torso. Now add ragged edges to the wings and more detail to the hair.

STEP 5

Use a pen to go over the lines that will be visible in the finished drawing and erase any pencil lines. Add detail to the dragon's wings and draw the end of the horn visible on the far side of its face. The top of the tail has sharp barbs and the sections can be seen on the underside. A bead of spit flying from its mouth is a nice finishing touch.

STEP 6

Add the base coloring as shown. An all-over gray would not have made the most of this character. Notice how different, yet complementary colors have been used, most significantly for the chest plate and the underside of the tail.

STEP 7
Use lighter shades to add highlights to your drawing and darker colors for the shadows.

WARRIOR MONK

The warrior monks of feudal Japan were both Buddhists and respected fighters. In manga stories they are often depicted as travelers whose message of peace can quickly change to armed aggression if the need arises.

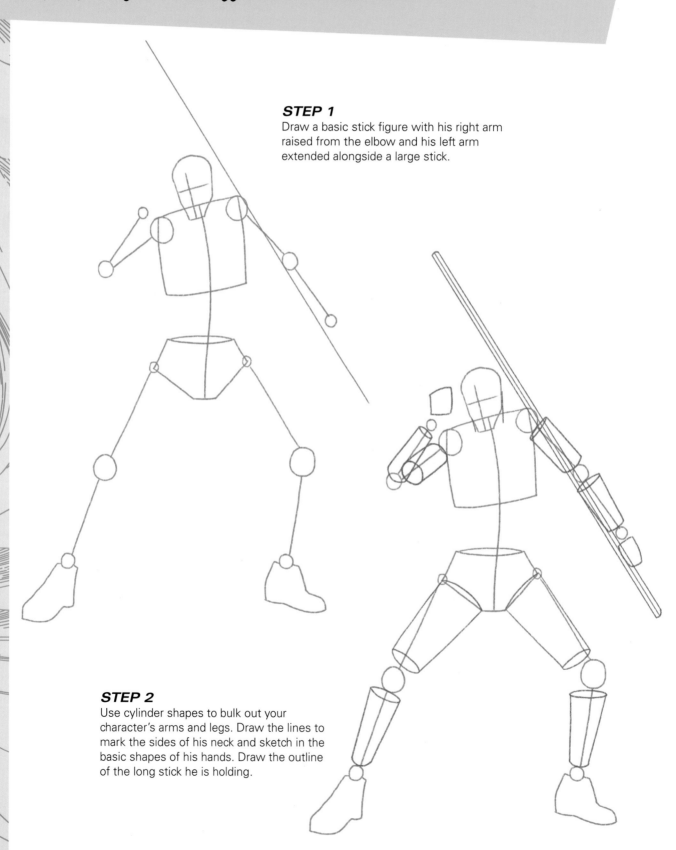

STEP 1
Draw a basic stick figure with his right arm raised from the elbow and his left arm extended alongside a large stick.

STEP 2
Use cylinder shapes to bulk out your character's arms and legs. Draw the lines to mark the sides of his neck and sketch in the basic shapes of his hands. Draw the outline of the long stick he is holding.

STEP 3
Add your character's basic anatomical details and facial features. He has muscular arms and legs and a square chin. Now draw his hands – the fingers of the right are raised above his head and his left fingers are wrapped around the stick.

STEP 4
Draw the monk's huge hat, which will be in front of the stick. Add shadows around his eyes where they are shaded by the hat. Draw his clothing, including a long cloak, wristbands, and boots.

STEP 5
Use your lining pen to go over the lines that will be visible in the finished drawing, and erase any pencil lines. Add details to the monk's muscles, clothes, hat, belt, wristbands, and boots, and the shadow under his chin.

STEP 6
The sharply contrasting colors match the dramatic pose, giving this character dynamism and presence.

ARTIST'S TIP

To get vibrant colors in your painting, try adding more than one coat of color to your character. Slowly build up the tone until you get the hue you are looking for.

STEP 7

Use darker color to add shading, which will give depth to your character.

MAKING MONSTERS

Manga teems with monsters and beasts of every description. These amazing creatures can spring from wherever your imagination takes you, as you can easily take basic human figures and turn them into monsters.

Beastly bodies

Most things in nature grow in a way that is based on symmetry. This means that when we see something that is lopsided or asymmetrical we tend to regard it as odd and somehow wrong. You can use this to your advantage in designing a monster.

Using what we already know of anatomy, we can play with proportion to emphasize the power of a character. Here, large shoulders and forearms suggest brute strength, but because they remain symmetrical the image doesn't look too unsettling.

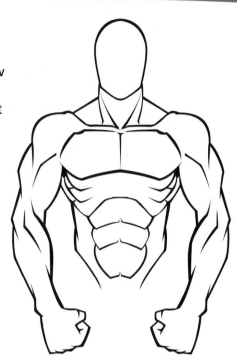

See how the additions we have made to a basic body shape have created something monstrous.

Place things such as eyeballs or mouths out of their natural position.

Introduce elements from other creatures, such as webbed hands and feet.

Try swapping hands for claws or long, spindly talons.

Horrible heads

The characteristics of the human face are so familiar that even slight changes to what we expect to see will help to bring out the beastly side of your creations.

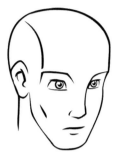

A basic human head is your starting point for creating something monstrous.

Shading can produce hollowed-out eyes and misshapen teeth.

You can change the shape of the skull and add horns.

A strong browline and outsized jaw will make your character look brutish.

Wings

Only slight adaptations are needed to transform a normal arm into a wing. The wing membrane is supported by "fingers" from the elbow and wrist. The hand becomes a talon.

This wing has similar pivot points to a human arm.

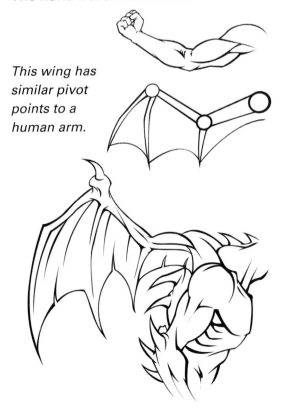

Time for tentacles

Multiple tentacles can be confusing to work with. The trick is to draw each one as a simple line before thickening them out. If you treat each strand as a three-dimensional tube, you will find it easier to visualize as it twists and overlaps itself.

MUTANT OGRE

Imagine a secret government agency carrying out horrific genetic experiments. What sort of creature would emerge from the lab? This mutant is an experiment gone wrong, with the left side of its body twisted into something truly terrifying.

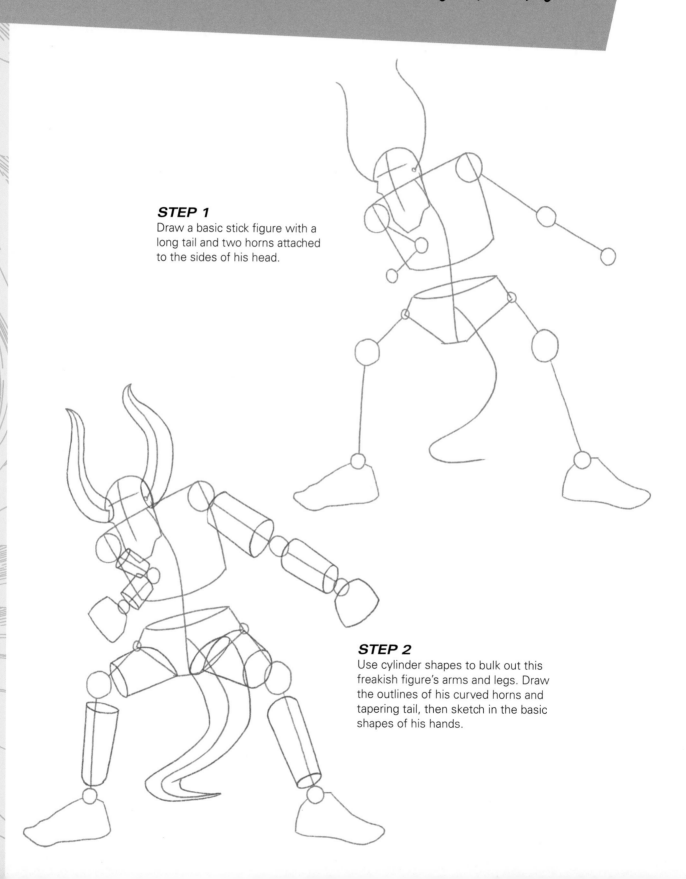

STEP 1
Draw a basic stick figure with a long tail and two horns attached to the sides of his head.

STEP 2
Use cylinder shapes to bulk out this freakish figure's arms and legs. Draw the outlines of his curved horns and tapering tail, then sketch in the basic shapes of his hands.

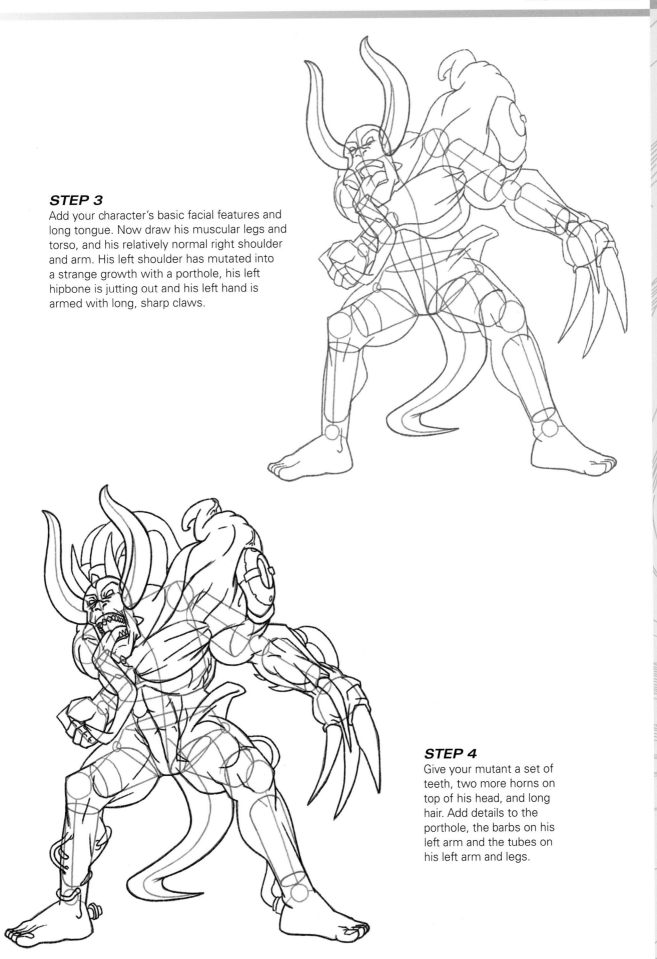

STEP 3

Add your character's basic facial features and long tongue. Now draw his muscular legs and torso, and his relatively normal right shoulder and arm. His left shoulder has mutated into a strange growth with a porthole, his left hipbone is jutting out and his left hand is armed with long, sharp claws.

STEP 4

Give your mutant a set of teeth, two more horns on top of his head, and long hair. Add details to the porthole, the barbs on his left arm and the tubes on his left arm and legs.

STEP 5

Use your lining pen to go over the lines that will be visible in the finished drawing, and erase any pencil lines. Add some initial shading and draw in the barbs at the end of the mutant's tail, then put the finishing touches on his body, face, horns, hair, and the tubes attached to his arm and legs.

● ARTIST'S TIP

The construction cylinders on the left arm are much larger than those on the right. They show how the mutation has warped the left arm.

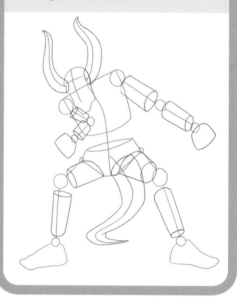

STEP 6

Add the coloring using lighter shades as shown. The contrasting colors used for the pipes and the arm panel ensure that we notice these vital features.

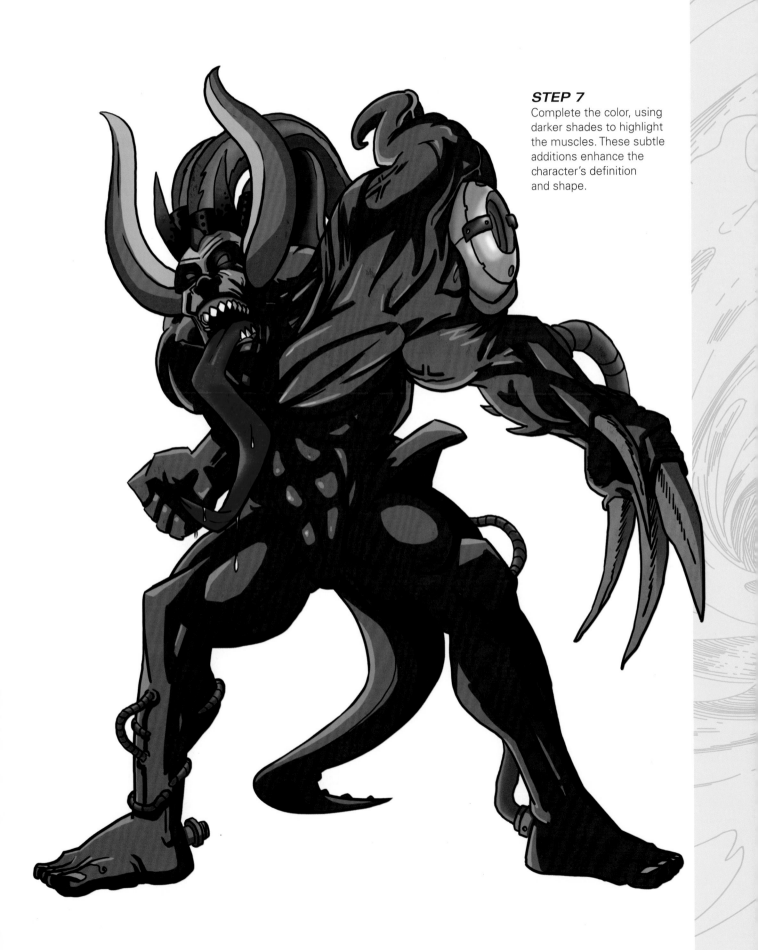

STEP 7
Complete the color, using darker shades to highlight the muscles. These subtle additions enhance the character's definition and shape.

GLOSSARY

barb A sharp point on a hook, arrow or similar object that makes it hard to pull that object out of a wound.

Buddhist Belonging to Buddhism, a religion from Asia.

charred Slightly burned.

debris Pieces of something that has broken apart.

element One of the basic substances which people used to believe made up the world: water, fire, earth and air.

ember A small item from a fire, glowing with heat.

feudal A system of government in which nobles owned the land and peasants worked on it in return for a share of the crops.

focus lines The lines drawn around a picture to emphasize its importance.

pact An agreement.

particle A very small amount of something.

porthole A small window on the side of a plane or ship, often round in shape.

socket A hollow into which something fits.

trajectory The path an object takes through the air.

FURTHER READING

Mastering Manga with Mark Crilley by Mark Crilley (Impact Books, 2012)

Ready, Set, Draw!: Manga by Ailin Chambers (Gareth Stevens, 2014)

Write and Draw Your Own Comics by Louie Stowell (Usborne, 2014)

WEBSITES

Due to the changing nature of Internet links, PowerKids Press has developed an online list of websites related to the subject of this book. This site is updated regularly. Please use this link to access the list: **www.powerkidslinks.com/um/fantasy**

INDEX